Holiday Histories

Independence Day

Mir Tamim Ansary

Heinemann Library
Chicago, Illinois

Customer Service 888-454-2279
Visit our website at www.heinemannraintree.com

Designed by Kimberly Miracle and Q2A Creative
Printed in China by South China Printing Company

10 09 08 07 06
10 9 8 7 6 5 4 3 2 1

New edition ISBNs: 1-4034-8887-8 (hardcover)
                                1-4034-8900-9 (paperback)

The Library of Congress has cataloged the first edition as follows:
Ansary, Mir Tamim.
    Independence Day / Mir Tamim Ansary.
        p. cm. -- (Holiday histories)
    Includes bibliographical references and index.
    ISBN 1-58810-223-8 (lib. bdg.)
    1. Fourth of July – Juvenile literature. 2. Fourth of July celebrations – Juvenile literature. 3. United States – History – Colonial period, ca. 1600-1775 – Juvenile literature. 4. United States – History – Revolution, 1775-1783 – Juvenile literature. [1. Fourth of July. 2. Holidays. 3. United States – History – Colonial period, ca. 1600-1775. 4. United States – History – Revolution, 1775-1783] I. Title.

E286 .A1246 2001
394.2634 – dc21
                            2001000073

Acknowledgments
The author and publishers are grateful to the following for permission to reproduce photographs: Alamy p. 20 (North Wind Picture Archives); AP/Wide World p. 24; Corbis pp. 28-29 (Firefly Productions); Culver Pictures p. 8; The Granger Collection pp. 10, 13, 15, 21, 25; North Wind Pictures pp. 11, 12, 16, 17, 18, 19, 22, 23, 26, 27; Photo Edit pp. 4-5 (Gary A. Conner), 6-7 (Jeff Greenberg); Super Stock p. 14.

Cover photograph reproduced with permission of BL Images/Alamy.

Every effort has been made to contact copyright holders of any material reproduced in this book. Any omissions will be rectified in subsequent printings if notice is given to the publisher.

Disclaimer
All the Internet addresses (URLs) given in this book were valid at the time of going to press. However, due to the dynamic nature of the Internet, some addresses may have changed, or sites may have changed or ceased to exist since publication. While the author and publisher regret any inconvenience this may cause readers, no responsibility for any such changes can be accepted by either the author or the publisher.

Contents

Some words are shown in bold, **like this**. You can find out what they mean by looking in the glossary.

A Summer Holiday

Independence Day is our biggest summer
holiday. It is always on the fourth of July.
At this time of year, the days are long and warm.

Many families spend the holiday outdoors. They watch parades. They have picnics. Then, as night falls, excitement grows. Everyone knows what is coming—fireworks!

Celebrating Our Independence

Fireworks have long been a part of **Independence** Day. They remind some people of war. Our country won its independence by fighting a war.

Independence is another way of saying "freedom." Why did our country have to win its freedom? From whom? That story begins about 400 years ago.

Thirteen English Colonies

Before the 1600s, few **Europeans** lived in North America. Then a group of English people came to this land. In 1607 they built a village called Jamestown.

Captain John Smith was the leader of Jamestown.

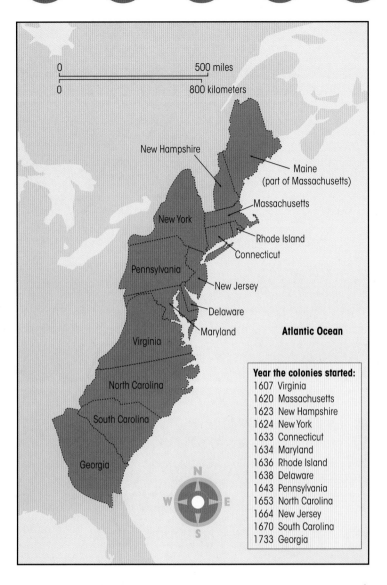

Map scale: 0 — 500 miles, 0 — 800 kilometers

New Hampshire

Maine
(part of Massachusetts)

Massachusetts

New York

Rhode Island

Connecticut

Pennsylvania

New Jersey

Delaware

Maryland

Atlantic Ocean

Virginia

North Carolina

South Carolina

Georgia

Year the colonies started:
1607 Virginia
1620 Massachusetts
1623 New Hampshire
1624 New York
1633 Connecticut
1634 Maryland
1636 Rhode Island
1638 Delaware
1643 Pennsylvania
1653 North Carolina
1664 New Jersey
1670 South Carolina
1733 Georgia

More **settlers** followed. They were **colonists**.
They thought of themselves as English, but they
lived here, far from their own country. Thirteen
English **colonies** formed in North America.

A Busy New World

The **colonists** did well in this new land. They grew **crops** and caught fish. They sawed trees into **lumber**.

What they could not make, they bought. They traded with one another and also with England. New towns grew quickly in this land.

Growing Apart

At first the **colonists** were **loyal** to England and its king. But England was far away. When the colonists needed help, they could not get it from England.

They took care of most problems on their own. As time passed, they felt less and less connected to England—or Great Britain, as it was called after 1707.

The French and Indian War

In 1754 Great Britain went to war with France. Part of this war was fought in North America. This part was called the French and Indian War.

Many Native Americans fought on the side of the French during the French and Indian War.

The **British** won the French and Indian War.
They forced the French out of North America.
But the war had cost a lot of money. It left the
British king in **debt**.

The King's Taxes

The **British** king was George the Third. He decided to get money from the **colonists** in North America. He ordered them to pay him many new **taxes**.

The colonists thought these taxes were unfair.
They had not **voted** for a war. The king's **debt**
was not their fault. The money would not be
spent on their needs.

Angry Colonists

In fact, the **colonists** had no **vote** in the **British government**. So why should they pay British **taxes**? They asked this question to the king.

King George did not want to answer this question.
He sent soldiers to keep the colonists quiet. The
colonists were forced to let the soldiers live in
their homes!

Trouble in Boston

In 1770 trouble broke out in Boston. On March 5, **British** soldiers shot five **colonists** dead. People in the **colonies** were shocked. This was called the Boston **Massacre**.

Patrick Henry (standing, left) gave a famous speech to a group of colonists on March 23, 1775.

The colonists began to see Great Britain as an enemy. They spoke of breaking away from that country. "Give me **liberty** or give me death," cried a colonist leader named Patrick Henry.

War Breaks Out

In 1775 a **British** general thought the **colonists** were planning to make trouble. He decided to take away their **gunpowder**. But the colonists knew he was coming.

Paul Revere warned the colonists that the British were coming.

Some colonists hid near the villages of Concord and Lexington in Massachusetts. When the British marched past, they started shooting. The Revolutionary War had begun.

Thomas Jefferson

The Declaration of Independence

What exactly were the **colonists** fighting for? A man named Thomas Jefferson put it into words. His statement is called the **Declaration** of **Independence**.

24

Jefferson wrote that people have a right to choose their own leaders. He said the colonists no longer wanted **British** leaders or their laws. This announcement was signed on July 4, 1776.

The Declaration of Independence was read to the public on July 8, 1776 in Philadelphia, Pennsylvania.

A Nation Is Born

King George refused to let the **colonies** go. He sent his armies to North America. The **colonists** fought back. They were led by George Washington.

British General Cornwallis (left) gave up to George Washington (center) in the last battle of the Revolutionary War.

The Revolutionary War lasted eight years. In 1781 the **British** were beaten. The colonists could now form their own country. They formed the United States in 1783.

Many People, One Country

Americans have come from many places. Our country has grown from 13 **colonies** to 50 states.

Together we have built one country. It belongs to no one except us **citizens**. Fireworks on **Independence** Day help us celebrate our freedom and pride in our country.

Important Dates

Independence Day

1492	Christopher Columbus first explores the Americas
1607	Jamestown is founded
1733	Georgia, the thirteenth **colony**, is founded
1754	French and Indian War begins
1763	French and Indian War ends
1765	The Stamp Act creates many new **taxes** for **colonists**
1768	**British** soldiers arrive in Boston, Massachusetts
1770	The Boston **Massacre** takes place
1775	The Revolutionary War begins
1776	**Declaration** of **Independence**
1781	General Cornwallis surrenders at Yorktown
1783	The Revolutionary War ends
1787	The Constitution is written
1789	George Washington is elected the first president of the United States

Glossary

British	people from the country of Great Britain
citizens	members of a country
colony	land owned or controlled by another country
colonists	people who live in a colony
crops	plants grown by farmers for food and other uses
debt	owing someone money
declaration	statement that announces something
Europeans	people from the continent of Europe
government	all the people who govern a country, state, city, or town
gunpowder	exploding powder used to fire bullets
independence	being on one's own; not under someone else's control
liberty	freedom
loyal	faithful to; ready to serve and follow
lumber	wood sawed into boards
massacre	killing of many people who cannot fight back
settlers	people who move to a new place to live
taxes	money that a government collects from its citizens
vote	make one's choice

Find Out More

Burke, Rick. *Paul Revere*. Chicago: Heinemann Library, 2003.

Landau, Elaine. *Independence Day: Birthday of the United States*. Berkeley Heights, NJ: Enslow, 2001.

Schaefer, Ted and Lola Schaefer. *Independence Hall*. Chicago: Heinemann Library, 2006.

Index

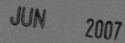